NATURAL DISASTERS

Photo Credits:

AP/ WideWorld Photos—End Pages; Pages 6-9, 12-29
Bettman Archives—Pages 10, 11,29
Superstock—Page 10
Kathleen Campbell/Liaison International—Page 11
Warren Faidley/International Stock—Cover; Page 6
Tom Carroll/International Stock—Page 12
Mike Howell/International Stock—Page 14
Horst Oesterwinter/International Stock—Page 15
Aaron Strong/Liaison International—Page 16
Gary Bigham/International Stock—Page 23
International Stock—Page 29
Patti McConville/The Image Bank—Page 22
Gamma Liaison/Figaro Magazine—Page 11
Porter Gifford/Gamma Liaison—Page 23
Steve Berman/Gamma Liaison—Page 23
Anthony Suau/Gamma Liaison—Page 28
Nat'l Center for Atmospheric Research/Nat'l Science
Foundation—Pages 28-29
Greg Vaughn/Tony Stone—Cover

Illustrations: Wayne Hovis

EYES ON ADVENTURE™

EXPLORING

NATURAL DISASTERS

**Written by
Stella Sands**

kidsbooks®
Incorporated

IN NATURE'S PATH

Earthquakes, tornadoes, floods—these are some of the severe acts of nature that affect our planet. What exactly makes them disasters? They are destructive, causing untold hardship and claiming thousands of lives every year.

TOP TWISTER

Tornadoes are spinning winds created by thunderstorms. Often called twisters, they come about when cool, dry air collides with warm, damp air. The Great Tri-State Tornado of March 18, 1925, was the deadliest ever in the U.S. It tore through Missouri, Illinois, and Indiana, killing 695 people.

▲When the Earth quakes, the ground bursts apart.

◀ SHAKY GROUND

Both earthquakes and volcanoes are part of the Earth's behavior. Our planet's surface is a rocky crust made up of a dozen or so plates. The plates move, sometimes causing such pressure that the land quakes, especially in an area of the Pacific known as the Ring of Fire. Other times, liquid rock can come up through spaces between the plates, forming a volcano.

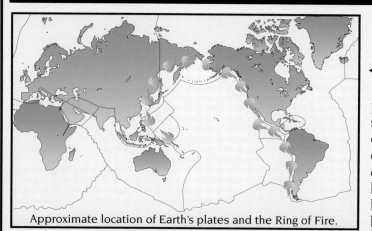

Approximate location of Earth's plates and the Ring of Fire.

SNOWBOUND ▶

A big snow, or blizzard, can cause a lot of damage and can shut a city down. However, snow can be fun and some people make the most of it.

◀ $$$

Hurricanes are formed from tropical storms. Unlike tornadoes, the winds of a hurricane can destroy a broad area and can last for days. Hurricane Andrew was one of the costliest in U.S. history, causing over $46 billion in damage. The storm left over 258,000 people homeless and tore through much of the Everglades National Park.

▼ BURN UP

Dry weather and soaring temperatures often make conditions in the western United States perfect for forest fires.

TO THE RESCUE ▶

Is there anything reassuring in the face of natural disasters? There is often a warning. Forecasters have modern technology at their fingertips—computers, satellites, radar, and more. Also, when a disaster does strike, people come together and help each other out, and professionals come to the rescue—firefighters, medical workers, and special disaster teams.

◀ RAGING RIVER

When it rains, and it pours, it sometimes floods. Imagine two months of rain, and the mighty Mississippi River overflowing its banks. In 1993, nine states in the Midwest experienced the costliest flood in U.S. history —$20 billion in damage was done and about 70,000 people were left homeless.

EXPLODING GIANTS

Volcanoes are sometimes called sleeping giants. They can rest quietly for decades or even centuries. But when they wake up, watch out!

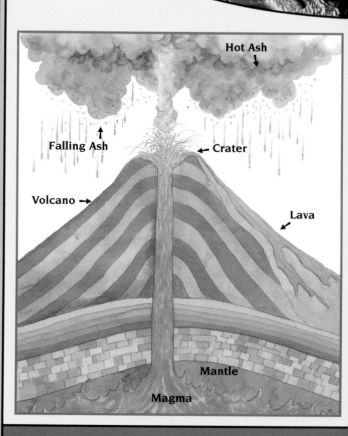

An eruption of ▶ Kilauea in Hawaii.

OVER THE TOP

The deadliest volcano ever to erupt blew its stack in Sumbawa, Indonesia, in April 1815. Lava and gases killed 92,000 people.

▲ A volcanic ball of fire.

BLAST FROM THE PAST!

One of the biggest volcanic explosions ever recorded took place on an island in Indonesia. On August 27, 1883, Krakatau volcano erupted, killing more than 36,000 people and destroying about 160 villages. It is estimated that the explosion was over 25 times more powerful than the largest hydrogen bomb ever tested!

HOT STUFF ▶

Hot liquid rock erupts from inside the Earth. There, in a layer known as the mantle, temperatures reach a roaring 2,200°F! The thick flowing rock substance is known as magma. Once magma comes out of the ground, it's called lava.

Hot Ash

Falling Ash

Crater

Volcano →

Lava

Mantle

Magma

8

MOUNTAIN TOPPER ▼

In this infrared aerial photograph taken from 15,000 feet by NASA, you can see the 1980 eruption of Mt. St. Helens. The volcano lost 1,300 feet off its top and caused 57 deaths—more than any other eruption in U.S. history.

CHECKING IT OUT ▼

Volcanologists are people who study volcanoes. They look for signs indicating the next eruption. They also venture out to study volcanoes in action and lava on the move.

SAVED BY THE CELL

About 30,000 people died in the eruption of Mt. Pelée on the island of Martinique in the West Indies in 1902. But many people survived. One was spared because the thick walls of his jail cell protected him from the blast.

▼ LAVA WILL TRAVEL

Lava stopped short of these homes near Mt. Etna in Sicily, Italy, and spared them from complete ruin. But lava can really move, swallowing whole cities and destroying all in its path.

▲ These Hollywood cameramen happened to be near-by when a volcano in Mexico erupted in 1943.

GOOD DEEDS

Although volcanoes do damage, they also cause soil to become more fertile and create entire islands, such as Hawaii and Iceland. Also, there are useful volcanic materials, such as pumice and basalt.

9

LOST CITIES

Almost 2,000 years ago in a Roman city known as Pompeii, a great disaster was about to happen. On the outskirts of town was Mt. Vesuvius. Many people lived near this lovely volcanic mountain. Some farmed its land. Little did they know that the volcano was ready to blow its top!

▲ BLOW UP

On August 24, A.D. 79, Mt. Vesuvius erupted. Within hours, Pompeii was buried under 6 to 20 feet of ash and spongy rock, called pumice. Forgotten, Herculaneum was destroyed by a super hot river of lava. Both cities were not to be discovered for many centuries.

▼ STOPPED DEAD IN THEIR TRACKS

People from Pompeii were buried as they tried to escape. Over the years as they deteriorated, the bodies left a space in the hardened volcanic rock. Archaeologists (scientists who study past cultures) discovered these spaces and poured liquid plaster down into the rock. They later dug out the hardened plaster, creating a permanent record of the fallen victims.

◀ VIEW OF VESUVIUS

Vesuvius has been painted by many artists. This painting depicts people fleeing Pompeii. Citizens who actually survived the rain of volcanic ash returned to their city to scavenge for riches. In later centuries people continued to pillage, and many archaeological treasures ended up in museums.

▲ A house in Pompeii.

◀ In Pompeii, the ovens from a baker's shop survived the volcanic eruption.

LOST AND FOUND

Houses and other buildings have been uncovered in Pompeii and Herculaneum, leaving a perfect time capsule of daily life almost 2,000 years ago. However, much remains to be excavated in Herculaneum. Work there has been more difficult than at Pompeii, because Herculaneum was buried in lava, which is much heavier than ash and pumice.

▲ The house of Poseidon in Herculaneum contains the best-known mosaic discovered in the ruins.

LOOKS CAN FOOL

Look out! Mt. Vesuvius can erupt again. It is, after all, an active volcano. An active volcano is one that is erupting or has erupted since the time that written records have been kept. The last really spectacular eruption of Mt. Vesuvius occurred in 1944, and in 1906 the volcano blew off the ring of its crater.

◀ Mt. Vesuvius and the remains of Pompeii in present-day southern Italy.

11

QUAKES

Like much of nature's fury, earthquakes are short-lived. But their destruction echoes for years. Earthquakes have been taking place since the beginning of time. And although scientists are better able to predict them today, earthquakes still cause enormous damage and great loss of life.

The roof was taken off this house during the 1994 earthquake in Los Angeles.

PURE DESTRUCTION

The Los Angeles earthquake of January 17, 1994, was the most destructive in U.S. history, killing 61 people and injuring more than 8,000. The loss in dollars was close to $20 billion.

DEFINITELY DEADLY
Fortunately, some earthquakes hit where few people live and work. Others, however, offer no such mercy. One of these deadly quakes occurred in Tangshan, China, in 1976. Registering 8.2 on the Richter scale, the quake killed 242,000 people!

▲ Workers rescued this man from a collapsed building after the 1994 quake in California.

DOUBLE TEAMING

The strongest earthquake in U.S. history struck William Sound, Alaska, on March 27, 1964. It measured 8.4 on the Richter scale. Following the quake came a giant wave from the sea. Called a tsunami (sue-NAH-me), the wave traveled at 450 mph and destroyed the town of Kodiak.

This geologist is examining a seismograph after an earthquake measuring 5.0 hit Los Angeles. The machine records movements in the Earth.

TAKING MEASURE

Charles F. Richter invented what is known as the Richter scale. It has been used since 1935 to measure the strength of an earthquake. Very few earthquakes register above an 8.0. If one does, it means there's a whole lot of shaking going on!

◄ A quake does more than shake the Earth. It breaks open water lines and brings down power lines, causing fires and floods.

HELPING HANDS

After the disastrous earthquake in Armenia on December 7, 1988, was reported on television, rescue workers from all over the world came to help. The quake, measuring 6.9 on the Richter scale, killed over 25,000 people, injured 15,000, and left 400,000 homeless.

JAPAN'S HORROR

Located on the Ring of Fire, where four out of five earthquakes occur, Japan gets hit hard by quakes. On January 17, 1995, a quake struck Kobe with a magnitude of 7.2 on the Richter scale, causing about $100 billion in damage.

◄ On September 1, 1923, an earthquake struck the Kanto Plain in Japan, leaving over 550,000 dwellings destroyed.

13

SHAKY SAN FRANCISCO

San Francisco, California, is a fun place to visit. There are cable cars and neat hills, a blue bay, and, beyond it, the Pacific Ocean. But, unless you like living on the edge, you may not want to live there. Sometimes tremors occur and there's little destruction. But when a big quake hits, the effects can be disastrous.

▶ Between quakes, the city enjoys a quiet, peaceful time.

▼ Search teams use dogs to find people trapped in the rubble of collapsed buildings.

The San Andreas fault lines.

Fires following the 1906 quake roared out of control, as the city's main water supply was cut off.

A MAJOR FAULT

San Francisco sits on the San Andreas fault—a 600-mile stretch where a crack exists in the Earth's crust. When the huge plates that make up the crust push into each other, and the colliding rocks can no longer bend, the Earth begins to tremble under the pressure and an earthquake occurs.

CITY IN CHAOS

In the San Francisco earthquake of April 18, 1906, more than 500 people died and over four square miles of buildings were destroyed.

Hotels, hospitals, and other buildings collapsed.

TWISTERS

They spin and race along the ground at speeds of up to 250 miles per hour, picking up anything in their path, including cars and trains. Tornadoes have even been known to pluck chickens, leaving the poor creatures featherless but unharmed.

WHAT IS IT?

It's a twister, a cyclone, a whirlwind! All these words are used to name a tornado, the storm with the fastest and strongest winds on Earth. But what *is* a tornado? It's a violently rotating column of air produced by a thunderstorm. Funnel shaped, the vortex usually moves over the land in a narrow path, staying in contact with both the thundercloud and the ground.

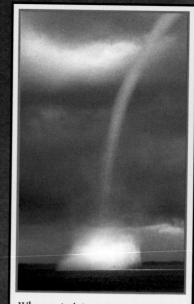

When a twister contacts water instead of the ground, it forms a waterspout.

ONSTAGE

Between April 3 and 4, in 1974, over 140 tornadoes touched down in 13 states and Canada. It was a lucky day, however, for some drama students at the local high school in Xenia, Ohio. They escaped to a hallway just in time—before two buses landed onstage.

◀ Destruction to Xenia

Most tornadoes in the U.S. occur in the Midwest. Kansas, Missouri, Oklahoma, and Texas make up a region known as Tornado Alley. Oklahoma is struck by tornadoes more than any other place on Earth.

LISTEN UP

Tornado season occurs in both spring and fall. If heavy thunderstorms are in your area, turn on your TV or radio. A tornado *watch* means that the thunderstorms could contain tornadoes. A tornado *warning* means that a tornado has actually been detected on radar or seen by people.

WHAT TO DO WHEN A TWISTER HITS

How do you stay safe when a tornado is hurling a barn from its foundation or stripping the roof off a house? Some people have fiberglass shelters buried in their backyards. Others take refuge in the basement.

OFF THE CHARTS

Tornadoes are rated from F0 to F5 based on the damage they do. A rating of F0 means that the damage was light. Maybe some windows were shattered. A rating of F5 means that the damage was "incredible," with houses and cars carried away. The scale, called the Fujita scale, was devised by T. Theodore Fujita, a physics professor.

An F2 can rip the roof off a house.

HURRICANES

They kill more people than any other storm. They uproot trees, flatten buildings, and cause floods. With winds of up to 220 mph, they devastate entire cities. Andrew, Camille, Agnes, and Gilbert—these are the names given to some of the most devastating hurricanes in history.

High tides caused by Hurricane Marilyn ▶ carried boats onto the streets in the Virgin Islands.

Much of the damage from hurricanes is caused by huge ocean waves blown to shore.

1954

It was not a good year for people living along the Eastern seaboard. In August, Hurricane Carol pounded the area. In October, Hurricane Hazel tore through the country, hitting Canada as well.

WHAT'S IN A NAME?

Hurricanes used to have only female names. But since 1979, hurricanes have been named for men and women. The first man's name to be used was Bob.

Swirling upper level winds

High altitude clouds

Cloud wall around eye

Rain clouds

Swirling lower level winds

Water

Eye

▲ BIG WIND

Hurricanes form over the ocean when warm air combines with cool air to create wind. If water is present and the wind is strong, a tropical storm forms. About half these storms become hurricanes.

INSIDE THE EYE ▶

A hurricane has a calm center, called an eye, which you can see in this satellite image of Hurricane Gilbert. Satellites help forecasters give early warning to residents and, therefore, help save lives. But satellites weren't around in 1900, when a hurricane hit Galveston, Texas, and killed 6,000. It was the worst hurricane disaster in the U.S.

FAST AND FURIOUS

In 1969, winds of Hurricane Camille reached 200 mph—the fastest sustained winds in a U.S. hurricane—as they pounded Mississippi and Louisiana.

▼ ALSO KNOWN AS

Hurricanes are called typhoons in the China seas and cyclones in the Indian Ocean. Regardless, they're usually deadly. Typhoon Ike devastated the Southern Philippines on September 2, 1984. More than 1,300 people died in flash floods triggered by the storm.

A ▶ U.S. soldier helps a young girl and her family get emergency supplies after Hurricane Andrew destroyed their home in Florida in 1992.

▲ Wreckage from Hurricane Hugo.

STORMY SPOT

In Bangladesh, a country in southern Asia, it's always a busy day for weather forecasters. Monsoons (heavy rains), floods, and cyclones (hurricanes) are just three of the severe weather conditions that plague the country.

▶ A tropical storm gathers over the Indian Ocean.

SO MANY PEOPLE
When a natural disaster hits Bangladesh, a great many people often die. One reason for this is that the population is so dense. There are more than 2,000 people for every square mile of land. In the U.S. there are only about 70 people per square mile.

A family takes to the roof to avoid the flood-waters that swallowed Bangladesh in 1988.

WATER, WATER EVERYWHERE
Flooding is the result of heavy rains. Up to 135 inches of rain can fall in Bangladesh in a year. Compare that with 38.6 inches, an average year in Seattle, Washington, a place in the U.S. that is known for being incredibly wet.

CYCLONES

Cyclones are responsible for thousands of deaths in Bangladesh. In November 1970 a cyclone, along with a tidal wave that followed, killed more people than any other hurricane in history. Over 300,000 people died! Water from the Bay of Bengal swamped the area with a wall of water more than 20 feet high.

▲ A cyclone practically destroyed this settlement.

KILLER ICE
What weighs over two pounds, is ice cold, and can kill? The heaviest hailstone on record. Ice balls killed 92 people in Bangladesh on April 14, 1986.

These people are crossing through floodwaters over a sunken bamboo bridge to collect drinking water from a well.

MONSTER MONSOON

The heaviest monsoon in 70 years hit Bangladesh during August and September of 1988. Over three-quarters of the country was flooded. Thirty million people were left homeless.

BIG-TIME TWISTER
On April 26, 1989, one of the worst tornado disasters in the entire world hit Bangladesh. Around 1,000 people died in Shaturia.

▲ Now surrounded by floodwaters, this farm has been hit by a cyclone.

21

IT'S SNOWING!

Snowflakes cover trees, lawns, buildings, cars, and roads with a clean-looking velvety blanket. What could be more enchanting? But snow can also be dangerous. When a light dusting turns into a storm, which turns into a blizzard, few people are thinking about beauty.

BLANKET OF WHITE

The most disastrous winter storm in U.S. history took place in 1888. For about four days, a blizzard dropped five feet of snow all along the East Coast. Over 400 people died, and damage was estimated at about $20 million.

Wind is part of the problem during a blizzard. It piles snow in drifts and makes it difficult for people to navigate through city streets or over country roads.

BOWL OF SNOW

The greatest snowfall in a single storm in North America occurred at California's Mt. Shasta Ski Bowl from February 13 to 19, 1959. Over 15 feet of white stuff fell. That's over twice the height of basketball star Shaquille O'Neal.

SUPER-COOL ART ▶

People always rise to the occasion when nature sends mountains of flakes. If conditions are not disastrous, some people like to make snowmen or go sledding or skiing. Then there are the more serious creative types. Here an artist in chilly Minnesota gets down to business sculpting a face of snow three stories high.

◄ AVALANCHE

An avalanche is an uncontrollable slide of ice and snow traveling hundreds of miles per hour. A volcano can cause an avalanche. The Mt. Saint Helens eruption on May 18, 1980, in Washington, caused 96 billion cubic feet of snow to go tumbling down.

▼ A snow-covered Mt. Saint Helens.

In 1947, traffic was at a standstill during the heaviest blizzard yet recorded in New York City.

▼ RECORD BREAKER

Unusual for New York City, streets were almost completely empty on January 8, 1996. The blizzard that hit caused the entire Northeast to come to a near stand-still. Schools were closed and businesses were shut tight.

In 1996, New York broke its 1947 record of 63.2 inches of total snowfall in one year with a chilling 75.6 inches.

FIRE!

It's true that people cause a lot of forest fires. Matches get thrown down on the dry forest floor, or a campfire is not extinguished properly. But nature sets its own fires, especially when the land is dry and the wind is blowing. In July 1994, in the western U.S., conditions were perfect for a fire. Lightning ignited trees, setting off a blaze that caused 240,000 acres to burn in 11 states. Fourteen firefighters died near Glenwood Springs, Colorado.

TALK ABOUT HOT!

It was 1871, the driest year in memory, and small fires were burning all over Wisconsin. Some got way out of control. In the forest fire that burned in Peshtigo, on October 8, 1871, about 1,200 lives were lost. Over 2 billion trees burned in what is considered the worst U.S. forest fire in history.

SMOKEY

His official name is Smokey the Bear. His official slogan is "Only *you* can prevent forest fires." In 1968, Smokey had become the most popular symbol in the U.S., beating out President Lyndon B. Johnson.

IN THE WOODS

In California, some homes are so close to the woods and forests that fires often overtake them. From October 20 to 23, 1991, a brush fire in Oakland destroyed over 3,000 homes and apartments, causing about $1.5 billion in damage.

LENDING A HAND

Over 10,000 firefighters from all over the United States came to help put out the 1988 fire in Yellowstone National Park. They cleared parts of the forest to create firebreaks, areas where there would be nothing the fire could feed on. But strong winds kept pushing the flames across the breaks.

GOOD AND BAD

Some feel that forest fires may actually be a blessing. As the forest floor gets cluttered with underbrush and fallen trees, a potential fire becomes more and more dangerous. A fire tends to clean up the area and enables new trees to grow. And although wildlife flees the area during the time of danger, animals return once the fire is out.

Helicopters and airplanes often assist firefighters by dropping water and other fire retardants.

▼ WALL OF FIRE

Yellowstone, one of the largest national parks in the United States, has over 2.2 million acres. In the summer of 1988, over 1.3 million acres burned—more than half the park! It was the worst forest fire in any of our national parks.

FIERCE FLOODS

▲ Flooding in northern California reached the roofs in 1995.

Rain is an essential part of our world. But when there's too much, we get floods and a number of other disastrous events. Rivers overflow and take houses and cars with them. Power lines go down, and fires get started. Then, mud may slide over the land.

During the flood in the Midwest in 1993, which left thousands of people homeless, farm animals and pets had to be rescued, too.

▲ Firemen are rescuing a man who went back to his flooded home in St. Louis to rescue his cat.

▼ The airport in Jefferson City, Missouri, was completely covered by water in the 1993 flood.

BROKEN DAM ▶
More than 2,200 people died in the Johnstown, Pennsylvania, flood of 1889—the worst flood in U.S. history. A 37-year-old dam broke, causing a 20-to-30-foot-high wall containing 20 million tons of water to careen through Little Conemaugh Valley.

IMPERFECTION
Almost a century after the Johnstown flood of 1889, a new flood-control system was in place. It was declared practically perfect. Not so! Another flood swept over the land on July 19, 1977.

DANGEROUS RIVER
Southeast Asia experiences a lot of flooding. The Yellow River in China has overflowed many times. Major flooding there has caused the death of millions. In one flood alone, in 1931, 3.7 million people died.

+3.5 t

IN A FLASH
Flash floods occur after heavy rains when the weather has been dry. This downpour causes lakes and reservoirs to overflow. Dry ground can't absorb the runoff fast enough.

In 1995, heavy rains flooded many European cities.

27

NATURALLY WACKY

When you think of natural disasters, you may think of earthquakes shaking down houses, floods covering the land, or tornadoes carrying off property. But some natural occurrences seem more wacky than disastrous.

A landslide buried this town in the Philippines after a volcanic eruption.

◄ Workers wade through a muddy volcanic aftermath in Colombia.

Heavy rains in California in 1995 created disastrous mudslides.

LANDSLIDE

Too much rain can turn soil to mud, and too much creates a landslide. Landslides can also be caused by earthquakes, which loosen rock and debris.

These kids have captured a few giant hailstones from a recent storm.

INCREDIBLE ICE BALLS

Sometimes perfect balls of ice, hail is one of those strange things in nature we're sometimes excited to see. But hail can be dangerous. In 1990, 60 people were injured by baseball-size hailstones in Colorado. It was a costly hailstorm, causing over $625 million in damage.

▼ REALLY BAD LUCK

Imagine being struck by lightning once. Disaster! Now imagine being struck by lightning seven times— and living to tell the tales. Former park ranger Roy C. Sullivan was struck in 1942 for the first time. Then, he was hit again in 1969, 1970, 1972, 1973, 1976, and 1977.

▼ One of many famous photographs taken of the dust bowl. Photographer Arthur Rothstein captured a father and his children running for cover as a storm of dust approached.

▲ WHALE OF A GALE

What is not a tornado or hurricane, but is not just a breeze? Strong winds known as gales. They shake whole trees and make it difficult for people to walk. These Japanese tourists got caught off guard in Paris by gusts of winds traveling over 80 mph!

DUST BOWL

What happens when you don't have rain? Drought. The longest drought of the 20th century took place in the U.S. in the 1930s. During 1934, dry regions stretched from New York to California. Much of the Great Plains was called the "dust bowl." There, topsoil blew away easily because it had been over-worked. Strong winds carried it around and created drifts of fine dust.

WHAT A DEVIL!

Tornadoes suck up anything in their path. When they travel over the desert, sand is the thing they pick up most. This swirl of grit is called a dust devil, and its name suits it.

29